The Joy Luck Club

BARNES & NOBLE® READER'S COMPANION™

Today's take on tomorrow's classics.

FICTION

THE CORRECTIONS by Jonathan Franzen
I KNOW WHY THE CAGED BIRD SINGS by Maya Angelou
THE JOY LUCK CLUB by Amy Tan
THE LOVELY BONES by Alice Sebold
THE POISONWOOD BIBLE by Barbara Kingsolver
THE RED TENT by Anita Diamant
WE WERE THE MULVANEYS by Joyce Carol Oates
WHITE TEETH by Zadie Smith

NONFICTION

THE ART OF WAR by Sun Tzu
A BRIEF HISTORY OF TIME by Stephen Hawking
GUNS, GERMS, AND STEEL by Jared Diamond
JOHN ADAMS by David McCullough

AMY TAN'S

The Joy Luck Club

BARNES
& NOBLE
B O O K S

EDITORIAL DIRECTOR Justin Kestler
EXECUTIVE EDITOR Ben Florman
DIRECTOR OF TECHNOLOGY Tammy Hepps

SERIES EDITOR John Crowther
MANAGING EDITOR Vincent Janoski

WRITER John Henriksen
EDITOR Matt Blanchard
DESIGN Dan O. Williams, Matt Daniels

This edition published by Spark Publishing

Spark Publishing
A Division of SparkNotes LLC
120 Fifth Avenue, 8th Floor
New York, NY 10011

ISBN 1-58663-858-0

Library of Congress Cataloging-in-Publication Data available upon request

Printed and bound in the United States

Contents

BARNES & NOBLE® READER'S COMPANION™

WITH INTELLIGENT CONVERSATION AND ENGAGING commentary from a variety of perspectives, BARNES & NOBLE READER'S COMPANIONS are the perfect complement to today's most widely read and discussed books.

○ ○ ○

Whether you're reading on your own or as part of a book club, BARNES & NOBLE READER'S COMPANIONS provide insights and perspectives on today's most interesting reads: What are other people saying about this book? What's the author trying to tell me?

○ ○ ○

Pick up the BARNES & NOBLE READER'S COMPANION to learn more about what you're reading. From the big picture down to the details, you'll get today's take on tomorrow's classics.

Oceans Apart

The Joy Luck Club presents the stories of eight women who face one another across vast cultural and generational divides.

○   ○   ○

LIKE EACH OF THE SUBTLE AND POWERFUL STORIES it contains, Amy Tan's *The Joy Luck Club* is not as simple as it seems. Yes, its emotionally riveting tales are powerful page-turners, and yes, its characters explode a broad array of stereotypes. But while *The Joy Luck Club* masquerades as a modest collection of stories told by a clique of seemingly ordinary Chinese mothes and their daughters, its cultural importance goes far beyond that. The novel makes us think differently—about women, about mothers and daughters, about Chinese Americans, and about what it means to be American. Tan's novel achieves something rare: it not only entertains us but explores profound social and cultural issues along the way.

The *Joy Luck Club* focuses on the relationships between women—relationships that are rife with conflict. The mothers and daughters of *The Joy Luck Club* fight as much as they hug, if not more so. They don't always support one another. Often, they seethe with rivalry, jealousy, and thwarted vanity. The novel isn't an unconditional celebration of women and their relationships. It also elaborates on female disconnections, hostilities, and rifts. The emotional landscape of Tan's novel is a sharp-edged place with jagged cliffs.

Although *The Joy Luck Club* is a universal tale, it also overturns a slew of specific cultural stereotypes. Gone is the stereotype of the obedient, docile, and submissive Asian-American girl. We find the women of Tan's novel—young and old—just as rebellious and strong-willed as their white

American counterparts. In a fit of anger at her mother, the young Jing-mei Woo shouts that having a Chinese mother is a kind of slavery—a sentiment we sense the other daughters share. Unwilling to be subservient but also unwilling to lose their beloved mothers, these young women display a rebellious spirit that makes their lives a constant tug-of-war between respect and rage. Ironically, the daughters' willpower emerges as one of the many legacies they inherit from their equally strong mothers.

The Joy Luck Club also enrolls us in a crash course in Chinese-American culture. Tan's novel aims not only to entertain but also to teach us a thing or two about what it's like to be a Chinese immigrant to the United States. It covers immense ground, stirring our imagination with tales of Moon Ladies, disastrous arranged marriages, and mah-jongg games. Ultimately, it restores the voices of a large group of American citizens previously silenced by a culture that chose not to pay much attention to them.

Perhaps most important, Tan's novel is a joy to read. Page by page, we find ourselves in her characters' shoes, reading about the lives of people whose stories we might never have heard otherwise. In looking at America, at family, and at the world through these new eyes, we come to understand the joys and terrors of leaving behind a familiar life and jumping into the American melting pot, of treading the razor's edge between starting life in a new land and honoring the traditions of the old.

EAST AND WEST

Tan's characters belong to two homelands, two sets of traditions, and two belief systems. In choosing both China and California as the settings for the tales of *The Joy Luck Club*, Tan highlights the connections and tensions between East and West that color the lives of every character in the novel.

For the Chinese-American women of *The Joy Luck Club*, the notion of homeland becomes muddled. Is it China or America? Can it be both, or is it neither? The novel zigzags back and forth across the Pacific, sometimes recounting events in Shanghai or Tai Lake in China, sometimes telling of daily dramas on Stockton Street or Waverly Place in San Francisco. Tan uses this shifting geography to show that her characters live their lives somewhere in the space *between* America and Asia—or in both places at once, even for the women who have never actually set foot in China.

In this relentless back-and-forth movement, we relate to the characters' own confusion.

Both the older generation and the younger generation in Tan's novel struggle to navigate two cultures. Perceptions of home and abroad sometimes blur. The aging mothers in the novel refer to Americans as *waigoren*, or foreigners—literally in Chinese, "people from outside country." The implications of this stubborn assertion are fascinating, for they force us to ponder our own concepts of insider and outsider. When speaking Chinese, Tan's older characters turn the tables and confer insider status upon themselves in a place where they are often the "other." The mothers call their daughters "you Americans," which muddles even further the distinction between native and foreigner. The daughters inherit a huge legacy of Chinese culture from their Chinese parents, yet often feel themselves to be American rather than Chinese.

> **Tan's characters engage** in a never-**ending quest** to locate and **define themselves.**

The women of *The Joy Luck Club*, like so many of us, find their identity in their place of residence. But since Tan shifts the geography of her novel so consistently, she gives a new twist to the idea of finding yourself—a major theme of growing-up or coming-of-age novels. Just like Louisa May Alcott's *Little Women*, another popular novel with almost exclusively female characters, *The Joy Luck Club* reminds us that growing up is a process of asking ourselves questions about our own identities and aspirations.

Tan's characters engage in a never-ending quest to locate and define themselves. Many of the stories in *The Joy Luck Club* focus on the tough lessons and growing pains of adolescence, on the stumbling blocks in the path from childhood to adulthood as the girls try to create and discover their identities as women. Yet these characters in the novel also face the added challenge of finding themselves on the map of the world. It's not just the younger women who must carve out their identities. In this alien culture, the older women endure a sometimes-grueling second birth.

The question of elusive identity is at the heart of this work. In stories like Ying-ying St. Clair's tale "The Moon Lady," a lost young girl in China expresses her greatest wish: to be found. We know that the narrator of the tale is now an older woman in California and we wonder if she did indeed find herself there. As beautiful and mystical as China appears in "The Moon Lady," girls can get lost there, just as they can in America. Forced to consider where in the world Ying-ying truly becomes herself, we find ourselves meditating on the meaning of identity and homeland.

BECOMING AMERICAN, STAYING CHINESE

In shining her spotlight equally on China and America in this novel, Tan makes us expect a comparison of the two countries. After all, three of the novel's seven primary narrators have lived in both countries. But if we expect a rah-rah praise of the American lifestyle contrasted with a portrayal of misery back in the far East, we have a surprise coming. The America that appears in *The Joy Luck Club* is by no means a paradise. Life in the United States challenges the narrators of the novel as much as life in China does, though in different ways. Tan's narrators never praise the U.S. at the expense of China. Nor do they paint a simplistic picture of a luxurious lifestyle in America that contrasts with the remembered difficulties of China.

True, the characters never forget that life in America is easier in material ways. In the first story, "The Joy Luck Club," Auntie Lin pats her stomach and purrs that she has become fat and happy in America. And indeed, some of the stories we hear of life in China before emigration tear out our hearts with their cruelty, shame, and degradation. "The Red Candle," for instance, tells of Lindo Jong's tragic past. Forced into a loveless marriage to a tyrannical and selfish man, she has to put up with an abusive mother-in-law to boot.

Yet the characters in the novel who have lived in China often recall the loveliness and lyrical beauty of their old homeland. China offers occasional hardships, but often joy, peace, and family togetherness as well. In "The Moon Lady," Ying-ying St. Clair paints a dreamy picture of the Chinese landscape, with the full moon overhanging the vast and peaceful Tai Lake where the story reaches its climax. Much of that gentle and lulling story focuses on a small girl's enjoyment of the party on the lake and the pleasure of celebrating with her extended family. China, in this story, seems almost idyllic, a true home and homeland, a paradise in the eyes of exiles. China and America that are intricate, three-dimensional places that the women of *The Joy Luck Club* wrestle with every day. We rarely find any of these women holding up either place as a romantic ideal. To romanticize something, one must often be distanced from it. Yet China, although half a world away, is with the women every day. We see in Rose's and Waverly's marriage problems that the characters suffer in America just as they did back in China—if more subtly.

We do find real gaps and disparities between China and America, however. The characters live simultaneously in a Chinese and an American world. As a result, we see double standards and parallel realities that overlap at times but never dovetail completely. For example, in "Rules of the Game," when Lindo Jong thanks the First Chinese Baptist Church for donating a chessboard to her son Vincent, her gratitude seems sincere. But later, in private, Lindo becomes critical and says that the children should throw away the chessboard—it has pieces missing, and if it wasn't good enough for the people who gave it away, it isn't good enough for her children either. Lindo displays two very different reactions, both of them real. She's torn between sincere gratitude and disdain—a pull that permeates *The Joy Luck Club*.

Tan often finds humor in the sometimes stark disparity between Chinese and American perspectives. As author, she aims not to mock or downplay one viewpoint or the other but simply to show us how huge the gap in perceptions can be. When Waverly Jong asks her mother what Chinese torture is, reporting that a schoolmate taunted her with accusations of Chinese cruelty, her mother Lindo hilariously takes pride in Chinese torture as yet another example of Chinese ingenuity and skillfulness. The American liberal, outraged at torture, confronts the elder Chinese woman

A classic look

The traditional dresses that the older women in *The Joy Luck Club* wear in China are known as *qipao*, Mandarin for "banner gown." Contrary to popular belief, they came into fashion only quite recently—relative to the thousands of years of Chinese history, that is—during the Qing (or Manchu) Dynasty of the late 1800s. Although the 1911 revolution in China saw the downfall of the Qing rulers, their banner gown survived and became a traditional outfit for Chinese women.

who takes pride in all things made in China. The clash may be hard to reconcile, but we find humor in it.

In their struggle to integrate—or at least strike a balance between—these two different traditions, the women of *The Joy Luck Club* juggle China and America in a cultural sleight-of-hand. While the daughters wish to respect their mothers' traditions, they subscribe to more American ways. Throughout the novel, the younger generation makes fun of the elders' wisdom, from their *feng shui* to their claims to prophetic or extrasensory knowledge. Yet in the brief tale that prefaces the section "The Twenty-Six Malignant Gates," a mother's prophecy comes true even as her daughter demonstrates her disdain for such foolery. The daughters in *The Joy Luck Club* may mock Chinese beliefs, but in many cases these beliefs hold their own alongside American common sense. In the end, we must be wary of ruling out either one completely.

The money for a trip to China that the elder women offer to Jing-mei at the end of the novel's first story powerfully symbolizes the intertwining of China and America in *The Joy Luck Club*—and in Chinese-American lives more broadly. With this ticket, the members of the Joy Luck Club not only offer Jing-mei the chance to visit her dead ancestors' country as a landmark of past lives, but also give her the opportunity to visit her *living* family—her long-lost sisters. In episodes such as this one, Tan reminds us that China is by no means dead and buried to the characters who have left it to move to America—it remains very much alive and kicking, always hovering over the present.

China is an omnipresent force for the women who have left it to live in the United States, yet it is equally vivid for their daughters. Throughout the novel, Tan time and again shows us the ways in which China continues to live for these characters and the ways in which they continue to live within it. She examines the power of ghosts—absent cultures, absent husbands, an absent continent. On a daily basis, the women of *The Joy Luck Club* walk in multiple worlds—worlds that they are sometimes able to synthesize and that, at other times, stand diametrically opposed. We walk away from *The Joy Luck Club* with a sense of culture as a living being with many layers, many faces, and many influences.

EXPLORING WOMEN'S LIVES

The Joy Luck Club is a deeply female novel. Each of the seven narrators and most of the main characters are women. The men in the novel, meanwhile, linger in the margins like ghosts. We meet the men as husbands and fathers and see them gather in their own group while the wives play mah-jongg. But nothing the men do has much lasting importance. We know little about the men's careers, but our ignorance hardly seems to matter, for it's the women who determine the quality of life for their families. The mothers are vocal about their daughters' choices of careers and husbands. They have strong opinions on what would constitute a happy life for each daughter. The men, on the other hand, have little to say on these important subjects.

Although men in *The Joy Luck Club* are sometimes fearsome, they rarely present any real threat to women. For example, in Lindo Jong's story of her disastrous marriage, "The Red Candle," the much-feared husband turns out to be more frightened child than tyrant—utterly harmless. In fact, the real monster in Lindo's story proves to be her iron-fisted mother-in-law. The mothers in *The Joy Luck Club* enforce the rules and the laws as they insist on everything from piano practice to proper humility in social interactions. The mothers, not fathers, impose penalties for those who violate the rules. In "The Moon Lady," the characters pray to a female deity, not a male one. We have no glimpse of a man's world in this book.

Mah-jongg, marriage, manners—these are all traditionally female realms. But here, women even dominate stereotypically male domains. In "Rules of the Game," Waverly Jong becomes a chess champion despite her family's assumption that her brothers, not her, will be the ones interested in chess. The Jong sons watch in astonishment as their sister takes home all the trophies.

This display of female power isn't confined to modern America—we witness the same in the China of a half-century before. In "Magpies," when the young An-mei goes to a Tientsin mansion to live with her mother, the new concubine of a rich Chinese businessman, the man only *seems* to be the head of the household. In fact, it's the three other wives—notably the manipulative Second Wife—who wield the power. They terrorize An-mei's mother, far more so than her husband. The husband appears in the story only as a source of money and prestige, a man who provides no love and no affection. The other women, however, have the power to make An-mei's mother's life a living hell.

Failed marriages abound in *The Joy Luck Club*. Even in cases when husbands are key figures in certain stories, they're often on their way out of the daughters' lives. As Rose Hsu Jordan tells of the dissolution of her marriage with Ted and Lena St. Clair recounts her disappointments with Harold, we witness an end and a beginning of sorts. Rose and Lena emerge as individuals as their roles as wives dissolve. Rose's decision to fight to get her house back and Lena's dissatisfaction with her stifling marriage affirm the power of both women. As the men disappear from Rose's and Lena's lives, Tan showcases the depth of the women's personalities all the more clearly.

The predominance of women in *The Joy Luck Club* celebrates women's insight and wisdom. The women are far more vibrant than the men, and their highly honed philosophies of life course through it. Men may seem wise initially, but it's consistently the women in the novel who drive home life's lessons. In Rose's story "Half and Half," the father and mother initially appear equally self-confident and optimistic, full of vitality and strength. But after the tragic loss of Rose's brother Bing during a family outing at the beach, the men and boys in the family withdraw—the boys read comic books, and the father is almost half-hearted in his search for his lost son. It's An-mei and Rose who carry on the search the following day. Ultimately, the mother's despair at the loss of her son drives the family to forsake Christianity. The Bible becomes a prop for a short leg of the kitchen table. In this tale, as in *The Joy Luck Club* as a whole, the women are the actors in the social, practical, and emotional matters central to their family lives. The men, largely passive, hover on the outskirts.

Mothers and Daughters

By telling and hearing each other's stories, Tan's characters reach surprising insights about each other and about themselves.

○ ○ ○

JING-MEI WOO

Jing-mei serves as our sensitive, feisty, funny guide through the world of mothers and daughters in *The Joy Luck Club*. Though seven different women tell stories in the novel, Tan makes Jing-mei both anchor and reference point for us throughout the course of the book. Jing-mei narrates one tale in each of the novel's four sections, more than any other woman. Moreover, Tan gives her the privilege of narrating both the introductory story ("The Joy Luck Club") and the concluding story with its moving climax in mainland China ("A Pair of Tickets").

In the final tale, Jing-mei uses the money that her aunties offer her in the first story and returns to China. We can't help but feel that her experience of returning to her ancestral homeland symbolizes the dream of reconciling past and present, America and China, for all the Chinese Americans in the novel. Jing-mei acts out the drama of being Chinese-American more graphically than any other character, which may account for many readers' impressions that she stands in for Amy Tan herself.

Jing-mei displays more daughterly devotion than any of the others in her generation. Only she among the daughters has lost her mother, and her grief and nostalgia for the absent Suyuan imbues her with a deep regard for Chinese motherhood—a respect that is perhaps the central force of the novel. Yes, the other daughters in *The Joy Luck Club* do show

9

respect for their mothers as well. But we often feel that their respect originates from an empty sense of duty—showing respect only because they're expected to—rather than from the same sincere and lively reverence for the older generation that Jing-mei offers. Yet it's only after she has taken her mother's place at the mah-jongg table that her eyes open to this group's strength. The other daughters may eventually appreciate their mothers as Jing-mei does, but she alone earns a seat at the table of the elders.

Jing-mei arguably experiences a sharper split between the Chinese and American worlds than any of the other characters. Other characters call her by her Chinese name, Jing-mei, as well as her American name, June. No other characters must respond to two different names. This arrangement leaves Jing-mei with the luxury—or perhaps the burden—of shifting between names, and by extension, identities.

In the novel's first story, when Auntie Lin calls Jing-mei by her Chinese name, Auntie Ying quickly corrects her, changing the girl's name to June. But surprisingly, Jing-mei / June informs us that she prefers being called by her Chinese name, adding that it's "fashionable" now. On one hand, we appreciate her interest in returning to her ancestral roots. On the other hand, we wonder how deep her commitment to China really is if she adopts her Chinese name simply to be stylish. All the second-generation Chinese daughters in the novel share Jing-mei's vacillation between American and Chinese identities, but Jing-mei alone engages with dual identities in her very name.

Jing-mei also suffers under the burden of parental expectations more graphically than any other character. The older generation of women, having left China with dreams of better lives for their children, expect their privileged daughters to strive and succeed where they had no opportunity to do so. Some daughters, like the chess champion Waverly Jong, are able—at least early in life—to satisfy their mothers' ambitions, to bring glory and honor to the family. But in this regard Jing-mei has failed, or at least hasn't blossomed into a glowing success story. Her relentless hours of piano practice culminate in a dismal recital full of wrong notes and maternal disappointment. Waverly implies that Jing-mei's work as a copywriter for an advertising agency seems less than stellar. Wincing at the shame these failures bring to her mother's eyes, Jing-mei offers dramatic proof that a mother's dreams can be a heavy burden indeed.

WAVERLY JONG

Waverly Jong seems at first to be the superstar of the novel, the embodiment of every Chinese mother's vision of a successful daughter. Even her first name, with its aristocratic white overtones, suggests that she was born to achieve wealth, glory, and a real place for herself in America. She's the only character in the novel named after an American location—a sign of her mother's insistence that she take root and thrive in the new country.

Waverly's glorious destiny appears to be realized in her gift for chess, which wins her local and then national attention. Local stores sponsor her and revel in her tournament victories. All the while, her mother looms behind her, exulting in her triumphs but determined to keep her daughter humble. Waverly tells us that she wins at chess because she loves to win. Her competitive impulse is formidable.

Many years later, we see the reemergence of this competitive streak when Waverly insists on reminding Jing-mei that her own job is more prestigious than Jing-mei's, that her hairdresser charges more, and so on. Waverly shows us that competition among those groomed for success can be a flaw as well as a gift. We have trouble liking Waverly as much as we like the other daughters.

Yet Waverly's fierce competitive spirit is also a testament to the strength and capability of *The Joy Luck Club* women. The fact that Waverly wins her astounding victories in the traditionally male field of chess shows us that this girl's abilities can rival and outdo any boy's. When we see Waverly come close to refuting Bobby Fischer's smug prophecy that no girl could ever become a grand master at chess, we cheer her on. Waverly shreds the stereotype of the weak and submissive Asian girl with a vengeance.

On the street where you live

In *The Joy Luck Club*, Lindo Jong proudly names her daughter after the family's place of residence at the time, San Francisco's Waverly Place. A small alley between Stockton Street and Grant Avenue in Chinatown, Waverly Place is renowned among architecture buffs for its striking buildings. The fire escapes are painted in bright pinks and greens, connected by railings in delicate Chinese patterns. While there are no tourist shops in Waverly Place, visitors can stop by the Tien Hou Temple, the oldest Chinese temple in the United States.

Waverly's mother, Lindo Jong, hovers behind her daughter's success. Her role is somewhat mysterious. Lindo doesn't teach her daughter any chess techniques—quite the contrary, as her hilarious advice that Waverly try to keep more pieces on the board next time shows how little Lindo understands the game. And Lindo's constant observation and sighing as Waverly practices chess probably interferes with her daughter's progress more than it helps. But still, when Lindo adoringly polishes her daughter's trophies, Tan hints that a stronger connection exists. As reluctant as Waverly would be to admit it, she probably wins at least in part to please her mother. When Waverly rebels against chess and briefly stops playing, her mother's heart breaks, and something in their relationship is damaged forever. Waverly's subsequent loss of talent seems linked—vaguely but irrefutably—to the broken relationship with her mother.

Waverly's later life hints at the price she has paid for being so focused on success. She may have a prestigious job at a bank, but she behaves with cruel rivalry toward her lifelong friend Jing-mei. Waverly may have it all, but she has lost some humanity in the process. Nonetheless, her second story, "Four Directions," restores some of her humanity. We watch as Waverly searches for true love with the non-Chinese Rich Schields after her disastrous first marriage. Lindo ardently praised Waverly's first husband—Marvin Chen, a Chinese golden boy who turned out to be a flake. But after this disastrous first marriage, Waverly finally learns the difference between her mother's wishes for her and her own wishes for herself.

AN-MEI HSU

An-mei exemplifies the forces of myth and spirituality more powerfully than any other character in *The Joy Luck Club*. While other mothers like Suyuan Woo and Lindo Jong concentrate on practical concerns like piano practice and homework assignments, An-mei's deep connection with Chinese lore and legend makes her a kind of spokeswoman of the ancient homeland. It turns out that her American spirituality, which emerges later, is equally fervent. Though in some ways An-mei appears less commanding than the other mothers, she wields a degree of feeling and wisdom that renders her, in some ways, the more impressive character.

An-mei's spirituality fuses East and West, combining Chinese Buddhism and American Christianity. She names her sons Matthew, Mark, Luke, and Bing: the sudden shift from the names of the Christian evangelists to a traditional Chinese name suggests that An-mei abandons Christianity and veers back toward her native spiritual traditions at a certain point in her life. But this return to Chinese spirituality may not be total, for An-mei retains some traces of Christian faith. The Bible that was once dear to her heart may now prop up the kitchen table, but she takes care to keep it clean. Her tale of the turtle that eats human tears and later hatches joyful magpies from its eggs showcases her ability to spin a Buddhist yarn. But the tale's themes of accepting pain and sacrifice in life aren't so different from the teachings of Jesus. In virtually every instance, An-mei mixes two faiths to create her own potent brand of spirituality.

The conflict between new-world psychology and old-world Chinese advice-giving is especially pronounced in An-mei. She's indignant that her daughter, Rose, would open up to a "psyche-atric" about her marriage problems but shy away from talking to her own mother about them.

> *"'Not know your own mother?' cries Auntie An-mei with disbelief. 'How can you say? Your mother is in your bones!'"*

For An-mei, problems must remain in the family. Deeply personal, such matters are not for strangers to hear. Her diagnoses are hardly scientific in the American sense: she believes in Chinese magic and speaks to her daughter about ghosts and demons in a way that Rose doesn't understand. Nonetheless, she speaks in a way that forces Rose to believe her mother. An-mei ascends to a sort of earth-mother status via her links with the gods of the unconscious and the underworld.

The first tale An-mei narrates is a family story set in China, which places An-mei as an important connector of East and West before the other characters in the novel. She points out this connection in geography as well as in experience. The story of her mother's marital dissatisfaction in the early twentieth century echoes the daughters' later stories of broken marriages in the late twentieth. An-mei's mother's fur coat, a bitter emblem of her newfound riches won at the cost of her integrity, reminds us of An-mei's daughter's struggle to maintain her own integrity during her divorce from her husband, Ted. An-mei's story reveals the cross-generational link between a grandmother's and a granddaughter's life experiences. She shows us that although history has brought many changes, family life and marriage trouble will accompany every generation, up and down the family tree.

For sheer strength in the face of grief, An-mei rivals even the amazing Suyuan Woo, Jing-mei's mother, who carries her babies out of Kweilin on foot. But An-mei's grief is made in America. Unlike Suyuan and the other mothers, it's in California, not China, that An-mei suffers intense and devastating loss. The death of her son Bing on a family beach outing—when, as An-mei puts it, they tried to act like the typical American family on vacation—has all the tragic grandeur of the grief-laden tales that come out of old-world China. As a result, An-mei's vision of America is starker than that of the other mothers. Whereas the others see their new home optimistically, as a place of advancement and betterment, An-mei experiences America as a place of pain and mourning.

YING-YING ST. CLAIR

The most fragile personality in *The Joy Luck Club*, Ying-ying manifests the damaged sense of identity that can result from a lifetime of sacrifice, loss, and hardship. In her first story, "The Moon Lady," she declares that she has lost herself. Her tale focuses on her girlhood, when she fell into Tai Lake in China and returned as an anonymous earth-wanderer, a child cut off from the little girl she used to be. Even when she returns to her family's bosom, we feel that a part of her has been lost forever in the water.

Although Ying-ying ends that story happily with a claim that she found herself in the end, her assertion doesn't quite convince us. She remains a sort of half-person, not quite all there. Her marriage to her Irish-American husband appears passionless, even at the beginning when she half-heartedly allows herself to be courted—and then Clifford St. Clair seems to purchase her more than woo her. We wonder whether Ying-ying has ever loved him, or he, her. Ying-ying's daughter, Lena, flatly recounts how her father gave her mother a new American name, Betty. We're stunned that a husband could so easily take away his wife's name—part of her heritage and identity. We're stunned, too, that Ying-ying lets this pass.

Ying-ying strikes us as something of a doormat. She herself admits a deficiency of selfhood later on in the novel. In her last story, "Waiting Between the Trees," she describes herself as a dead person, a ghost with no *chi* or vital life force to pass on to her daughter. She wishes for the strength to become a tiger and fight with her daughter to prove herself—but she fails to back up her resolve with any action. She remains shadowy and passive throughout the novel.

Ying-ying's docile, almost listless nature provides us with a source of perspective and wisdom. As if haunting the world of the living from a place beyond the grave, she calls into doubt the values that others—especially

"Now I must tell my daughter every-thing. That she is the daughter of a ghost. She has no chi. *This is my greatest shame. How can I leave this world without leaving her my spirit?"*

the materialistic younger generation of Chinese Americans—hold dear. In her first story, she speaks almost condescendingly of her daughter, Lena, sitting by her fancy swimming pool with a cordless phone (the quintessential prestige symbol of the 1980s) and a Sony Walkman. The material possessions that are signs of success and wealth for others are, for Ying-ying, just superficial toys that distract from higher questions of life, death, and spiritual meaning. She says that her daughter listens to her Walkman rather than listening to her mother. Ying-ying accuses her daughter, however subtly, of having allowed American materialism to override Chinese wisdom. She judges her daughter's materialist values quietly but harshly.

Ying-ying's emptiness becomes a kind of blank mirror that reflects others' faces and shows them for what they truly are. Her name itself means "Clear Reflection," and the images she casts often unsettle us. They display the ugly truth that others would prefer to deny. Ying-ying secretly knows that her daughter, Lena, is as lost as she is. She knows that both mother and daughter fearfully hide their true selves from the world, but she can't tell Lena so. While other mothers like Lindo Jong deal with their daughters bluntly and directly, Ying-ying prefers an indirect, even a slightly passive-aggressive approach. When she can't bring herself to tell Lena that her daughter's marriage is clearly on the rocks, she signals her disapproval by knocking a flower vase off a wobbly bedside table Lena's husband built. Ying-ying knows the truth that Lena cannot face, yet she can only express it indirectly.

LENA ST. CLAIR

Unlike all the other characters in the novel, Lena has a fully European name, one that doesn't advertise her Chinese background. By her name alone, she could be an English aristocrat as easily as a Chinese-American architect. As the daughter of an Asian mother and white father, she has a racially ambiguous appearance as well. She tells us that she has Asian eyes, but that her skin is too pale to be Asian. In short, Lena can't be defined or labeled as quickly as the other characters.

Lena's ability to "pass" for non-Chinese distinguishes her from the other women in the novel. The only biracial character in *The Joy Luck Club*, Lena belongs fully to two different cultures and two different worlds, not just by immigration but by blood as well. She thus has a singular insight into both worlds, which is something that no other character has. Seeing both sides at once from within and without, Lena serves as the novel's most astute commentator on the divide between East and West.

Lena's powerful tale "The Voice from the Wall" demonstrates her double-sided understanding of what it means to be Chinese-American. Her ability to judge both cultures with equal incisiveness is clear. When Lena recalls her mother's temporary insanity after the death of her infant son Bing, she compares her own family's hardships with those of an Italian-American family next door. Through the wall, Lena can hear clearly that the mother in the family beats the daughter. This parallel makes us think about grief and pain in two different cultures at the same time. The neighbor girl, Teresa, becomes a kind of mirror image for Lena: Lena imagines what it would be like to be Teresa and meditates on the question of who has the worse life — and which family has the unhappier household.

Lena's objectivity regarding cultural difference makes her an especially useful and fair-minded touchstone for us. Lena is the only Chinese-American character who we see empathize strongly and deeply with a non-Chinese person at a young age. She feels great pity and concern for Teresa as she climbs out the window, playing a trick to torment her mother. No other character ever has the empathy for a white person that Lena conveys here. Even Ying-ying and Rose display less gut-level sympathy for their white husbands. Because of Lena's ability to feel as strongly about whites as about those of Chinese descent, we trust her emotional perspective on both cultures.

> Lena serves as an astute commentator on the divide between East and West.

Lena's sympathy for Teresa is a powerful reminder that sadness afflicts people regardless of ethnicity and that family trouble is an equal-opportunity woe. While other characters often voice the opinion that Chinese people display more talent, heroism, or determination that white Americans, Lena gives us instead a view of the human experience as a whole. While someone like Jing-mei may feel that her white schoolmates had an easier time with their mothers than she did, Lena knows better — she has seen first hand that *all* mother-daughter relationships can be problematic. When Lena asks herself which household is more miserable, she's unable to answer the question because she sees unhappiness and happiness in both.

But Lena *can't* see or accept certain aspects of her own life, like her marital dissatisfactions. Her marriage to Harold is more like a business partnership than a union of love. The couple tries to keep on course through a strict bookkeeping and accounting system that seems more appropriate to a corporate boardroom than a marriage. When we see this arrangement, we suspect that the thoroughly American Lena may be trying extra hard to avoid the stereotype of the "kept woman" that traditionally beset many Chinese women, such as An-mei's mother. Those women were bought and paid for, but we sense that Lena is determined to avoid even the remotest semblance of that fate by paying her own way, down to every last penny. But only her mother, Ying-ying, can see that Lena has gone too far, that where love should be there is only a financial agreement. In the end, Lena's American efficiency needs a little of her mother's Chinese wisdom to balance it.

Between Continents

Tan's women juggle two worlds and two sets of rules in trying to reconcile Chinese identity with American expectations.

○　○　○

What attitudes do the Chinese-American daughters in the novel have about traditional Chinese culture? Do they respect it? Or have they left it behind?

"THE DAUGHTERS MAY BE AMERICANIZED, BUT THEY STILL CARRY A DEEP RESPECT FOR THE CHINESE CULTURE OF THEIR ANCESTORS."

Though the daughters are frequently skeptical of their mothers' intuition, we ultimately feel that mother does know best. The daughters may roll their eyes, but in the end, they usually have to admit that their mothers are savvier than they expected.

Lena St. Clair provides a perfect example. When she first shows her mother the renovated house she and her husband, Harold, have just bought, she objects privately to her mother's mean-spirited criticism of the house's wood floor and sloped ceiling. Lena sees her mother as overly negative, unable to appreciate her daughter's new dream home, too selfish to give Lena the moment of approval that she craves from her mother. But in fact, Lena's mother, Ying-ying, is disappointed not in the house itself (as Lena believes), but in the crumbling domestic union that the house symbolizes. Ying-ying senses more clearly than Lena the problems in Lena's marriage. She criticizes the house as her only way to voice that intuition. Ultimately, as Lena's marriage falls apart, the older woman appears more clued-in than the hip young daughter.

The mothers in *The Joy Luck Club* repeatedly employ traditional Chinese prophecy and soothsaying. It often turns out to be quite accurate, however ludicrous it may initially appear to us and to their daughters. All the stories in the section entitled "The Twenty-Six Malignant Gates" demonstrate in one way or another the mothers' mysterious sixth sense about dangers to their children. The mothers seem to have inherited this intuitive knowledge as a Chinese cultural legacy, one that their daughters tend to scorn—but only until they learn better. The anecdote that prefaces "The Twenty-Six Malignant Gates" tells of a girl whose mother warns her not to ride her bicycle around the corner. The skeptical girl asks on what authority the mother issues such grandiose warnings. When her mother says that the authority is the ancient Chinese book of wisdom

"I used to believe everything my mother said, even when I didn't know what she meant."

The Twenty-Six Malignant Gates, the girl dismisses it as nonsense—and then falls off her bicycle immediately. In *The Joy Luck Club,* we can mock the wisdom of the ancients, but it always has the last word.

Jing-mei's eye-opening trip to China at the end of the novel provides a powerful symbol of the appreciation for China that the young generation develops. When Jing-mei finally visits the country she has only heard of dreamily for a long time, we feel that she finally learns something definitive—and quite positive—about her ancestral homeland. In the first story of the novel, Jing-mei knows China only as a hodgepodge of tall tales about moon goddesses and old women's memories of torturous arranged marriages. But by the end of the final story, when Jing-mei has arrived in China at last, we see her amazed by the marble lobby of the hotel and by its mini-fridges filled with Bacardi and Cadbury chocolate bars. She thinks to herself that this is a far cry from the Communist squalor she previously imagined, and we realize that China has impressed her.

But it's the emotional discoveries rather than these material discoveries that make Jing-mei's Chinese trip so successful. Her tearful, gratifying reunion with her long-lost sisters is all the proof we need of the wisdom of the old Chinese women who bought her the ticket. When the old women first propose the trip, Jing-mei is astonished and perplexed, wondering what on earth she could get out of a visit to a country that she has never seen, that she feels no ties to. Though Jing-mei doesn't say so directly, we sense that she sees the old mah-jongg players' idea as a madcap exercise in outworn nostalgia, the folly of some senile old women. But by the end, when Jing-mei tearfully embraces her relatives in China and acknowledges that they all look like their mother, we believe—as she does too—that the old Chinese women knew what they were talking about from the start. In the end, the daughters realize that their mothers' traditional wisdom overcomes their own seemingly modern practicality, proving itself right on target.

"THE DAUGHTERS ARE OVERWHELMINGLY CRITICAL OF THEIR MOTHERS' TRADITIONS, EVEN AT THE END."

Even though their mothers are sometimes right, the daughters in *The Joy Luck Club* remain skeptical of many aspects of their mothers' old-world culture. Listening to her mother tell the story of her feasts and mah-jongg games in Kweilin, Jing-mei remarks that the whole narrative sounds more like a fairy tale than history. She says that the ending of the story always used to change, as if her mother's memories of China were pure flights of fancy rather than actual experiences. Details, names, and whole endings of stories change seemingly at random, leading Jing-mei to regard with suspicion everything her mother says. We may share her feeling that the centuries-old oral traditions passed on from mother to daughter, and all the accumulated lore and wisdom they convey are little more than well-intentioned fictions. They may have entertained and instructed generations back in the Old World, but they have little value in the modern world of America.

In real life, Tan herself is not unlike the daughters in her novel. Not surprisingly, she puts certain traditional views that come naturally to the older generation under an especially sharp knife. Tan gives the mothers' old-fashioned pride in China's greatness in all skills an ironic send-up when we hear Lindo Jong asserting the greatness of Chinese torture. Here Tan clearly mocks the Chinese pride—perhaps arrogance—that Suyuan, Lindo, and other Chinese mothers in the novel occasionally display. There may be centuries of history behind their attitude, but Tan does not

> *"And then I decided.*
> *I didn't have to do what my mother*
> *said anymore. I wasn't her slave.*
> *This wasn't China."*

hesitate to dissect it. The daughters in *The Joy Luck Club* repeatedly denounce the sometimes dictatorial nature of traditional Chinese parenting. In her story "Two Kinds," Jing-mei Woo refuses to heed her mother's orders to practice the piano one day: "And then I decided. I didn't have to do what my mother said anymore. I wasn't her slave. This wasn't China." For Jing-mei, childhood in America means freedom, whereas traditional-style Chinese childhood is tantamount to enslavement.

Sometimes, in their drive to encourage success in their children, the mothers in *The Joy Luck Club* parade their children's accomplishments like glamorous accessories. The mothers sometimes appear less concerned with the happiness of the children than with using the children's talents to make rival mothers envious. Through her younger characters, Tan scrutinizes multiple aspects of Chinese motherhood.

At times, Tan seems to mock certain Chinese spiritual traditions. We sense skepticism in Tan's portrayal of the ancient Chinese practice of *feng shui*, for example. Now rather popular in the U.S. today, this theory of household layout comes under question—and even overt ridicule—in Lena St. Clair's story "The Voice from the Wall." Lena's mother, Ying-ying, paranoid about her pregnancy and dissatisfied with the family's new apartment, frantically rearranges the furniture day after day. She seems unable to voice her worries directly, so even her caring husband can't figure out what her compulsive behavior means. She makes so many changes to the layout of her home because she feels she can't talk about her feelings or make any active changes in her own life.

But rather than portray *feng shui* as a sophisticated tradition and practice, as many Americans have come to see it today, Tan puts a different slant on the ancient Chinese art. In Ying-ying's case, she frames it as the obsessive behavior of a half-crazed woman. In this story, *feng shui* horrifies and shames Ying-ying's daughter, Lena. Chinese traditions may have been effective in ancient China, but in most cases in the novel we feel that, in modern San Francisco at least, other approaches to life work better.

The Chinese tradition of arranged marriage is another target of the younger generation's criticism and scorn. This custom strikes many of the daughters—and probably most readers—as unthinkable and arcane. "The Red Candle," Lindo Jong's horrendous tale of being married off to a petty tyrant husband who doesn't love or desire her, provides yet another example of Tan's determination to cast light on the unsavory aspects of traditional Chinese culture. Though Lindo slyly gets the better of her husband in her story, the fact remains that marriage seems like slavery in her portrayal of it. Ying-ying St. Clair puts a similar spin on marriage in her own story: she all but admits that she didn't really love the man who brought her to America. Chinese girls of an earlier time sought protection, not love or personal fulfillment, from their marriages—and their daughters are quick to judge them for it.

"IN MOST CASES, THE DAUGHTERS ARE ABLE TO STRIKE A BALANCE BETWEEN A CRITICAL PERSPECTIVE ON CHINESE TRADITION AND A REVERENCE FOR IT."

While Tan does gently mock traditional Chinese beliefs, *The Joy Luck Club* ultimately affirms the wisdom and perspective of the older generation of Chinese women steeped in those beliefs. Although the younger, Americanized set sometimes dismisses their old-world mothers, they eventually live their lives according to their mothers' advice. Although they do so quietly, the daughters affirm the traditional wisdom they are too proud to praise outwardly.

The crumbling of Rose's marriage is one instance in which a daughter is able to consider and benefit from her mother's advice. Rose neither obeys An-mei nor disobeys her but indirectly mixes her mother's insights and intuitions with her own as she copes with her imminent divorce. We sense something shallow in An-mei's counsel, however. On the one hand, An-mei seems overly conventional in her opinions on her daughter's marriage: she originally opposed Rose's engagement to a white man, and now she opposes Rose's breakup with him.

At first, we suspect that social propriety drives An-mei's feelings more than any concern for her daughter's emotional happiness. An-mei's analysis of the situation is limited by her personal involvement and by the profound weight she places on family honor. Indeed, An-mei can't comprehend why Rose sees a psychiatrist (or "psyche-atric," as she calls it). After all, how could a stranger's opinion be more valuable than that of one's mother? As readers, we are more sympathetic to Rose's need for professional advice and an outsider's perspective.

Each of the **daughters** is slow to **realize** that mother **sometimes** knows **best.**

As it turns out, though, An-mei's grasp of Rose's emotional state is actually quite keen. Indeed, An-mei gives Rose some useful words of wisdom that Rose first rejects but later absorbs. An-mei shows surprising insight into Rose's relationship with her husband in her comment that Ted does "monkey business" with another woman. Rose initially rejects this idea as absurd, for she can't picture her cold-blooded husband doing anything so passionate. She even pokes fun at her mother's imagery: the idea of Ted bouncing around on the bed like a monkey during his shenanigans with this imagined other woman is laughable. But later, when Rose discovers that Ted indeed has another woman in tow, she realizes her mother was right.

Ultimately, Rose discovers that she has misunderstood her mother's attitude toward Ted. She realizes that her mother isn't urging her to shut up and accept marital woes as her due, but rather telling her to fight for her rights. While Rose initially believes An-mei counsels wimpy husband-fawning, in fact her mother advocates a strong feminist position and thinks she should "speak up," as she tells Rose on the phone. In the end, Rose listens. She informs Ted that, after the divorce, she intends to keep the beloved house that she's thus far assumed she must surrender. In this case, a Chinese mother's wisdom works in an American context. Rose maintains her independence while benefiting from her mother's advice.

While each of the other daughters has her own unique relationship with her mother, they all, like Rose, are slow to realize that mother sometimes knows best. Waverly, for instance, rebels against her mother's encouragement of chess practice only to discover in the process she loses her talent forever. While she never expressly admits that her mother was right all along, we feel it. Similarly, Jing-mei at first chafes at her mother's constant nagging about piano practice and rebels by practicing halfheartedly. But in the end, after her mother bequeaths the piano to her, Jing-mei renews her interest in it enough to have the piano tuned. As her fingers wander over the keys, she realizes that she may sincerely want to play the piano after all. What at first seemed like an oppressive maternal order later emerges as a mother's sixth sense about what might be a fulfilling activity for her daughter.

Lena sees her mother's wisdom after initially dismissing her mother's opinions as irrelevant. At first, Lena disentangles herself from the maternal forces in her life to a greater extent than any other daughter in the novel. In childhood, she seems distant from her mother, whose loss of a son drives her half-mad with grief. During this time, Lena treats Ying-ying more as a household embarrassment than as a potential source of guidance and advice. By the novel's close, Ying-ying communicates an observation that Lena can't face herself: that Lena's marriage can't hold up much longer. In allowing a vase to fall off a shoddily made table in Lena's home—a table that Lena's husband has made—Ying-ying drives home the point that she dares not state plainly: things are falling apart in this home, and Lena should face the facts.

It's undeniable that Tan shines a humorous light on the Chinese mothers in *The Joy Luck Club*. These ladies often seem overly fussy, unenlightened, dictatorial, or vain. But ultimately, Tan's gentle satire highlights the value that these women have in their daughters' lives. They strike us as comical enough to be human and real, but they're by no means lightweights: they have faced serious crises in their own lives. They have enough life experience to be voices of authority. The mothers often can't communicate their wisdom directly—their daughters must translate the Chinese sensibility to an American one and apply their mothers' insights to their lives in their own way. In the end, the daughters manage a compromise. They neither slavishly follow their mothers' directives nor ignore them, but adapt them creatively and independently.

Do the characters view China or America as the better place to live?

"CHINA HAS ITS DRAWBACKS, BUT ALSO APPEARS TO BE A PLACE OF SPIRITUAL RICHNESS AND CLARITY IN A WAY AMERICA ISN'T."

The mythical dimension of China is a consistent presence in every story set there. We feel its larger-than-life drama and the depth and extravagance of its offerings. In the stories the Chinese mothers narrate, colors appear brighter in China than in America, emotions appear stronger, and fate appears more extreme. Life may be materially satisfying in San Francisco, where everyone lives comfortably and finds lucrative work. Yet it can be dull compared to the adventures in the stories about China.

In China, people seem spiritually attuned in a way that they aren't in the United States. In "The Moon Lady," set on Tai Lake in China, everyone in the story knows that the goddess of the moon has the power to grant every girl's secret wish. This myth may seem childish, but in fact it demands a great deal of spiritual self-awareness to ask what one wishes for more than anything else. Indeed, the supposedly sophisticated American daughters in the novel often can't muster this self-awareness or come to grips with their own truest desires. Lena and Rose, for instance, don't know what they want. They vacillate in their private feelings about their marriages in a way that the little girl gazing at the moon goddess in China never does. Indeed, both Lena and Rose need their mothers to help tell them what they wish for in their lives. America may be the land of "psyche-atrics," but the therapists don't do much good. Where there is clarity in Tan's China, confusion abounds in her America.

Home cooking

Dim sum is a Cantonese food tradition from southern China, translating as "touching your heart." In China, dim sum was sampled mainly in teahouses, with an astounding variety of dishes, including steamed shrimp and pork dumplings, deep-fried egg rolls, and green peppers with shrimp fillings. The selection of dim sum varies seasonally and is prepared with equal attention given to color, fragrance, taste, and shape.

Everyday life in China bubbles over with drama. While the narrators present life in America as dull and prosaic, life in China, though sometimes oppressive and threatening, is never boring. The contrast between the humdrum United States and the vibrant and colorful Kweilin and Shanghai lingers powerfully in our memory. In California, mothers nag their daughters to practice the piano. In China, mothers flee cities with a daughter under each arm, making life-and-death decisions along the way. In the U.S., a prospective mother-in-law, such as Ted Jordan's mother, gently sends polite hints that the fiancée may not be good enough for the son to marry. In China, Lindo's mother's mother-in-law, Huang Taitai, is a fierce, manipulative woman who remorselessly spews venom at the new bride. While the human emotions we see in characters in the two countries may not be so very different, the contrast in the ways they're expressed—with operatic grandeur in China, and modest drabness in America—could scarcely hit us any harder.

People in the China of the novel attain an understanding of self more quickly than do people in the U.S. The truth about one's life that comes to light instantly in China dawns slowly in America, where people spend years being dazed before they accept the reality of their situations. In California, women like Lena and Rose indecisively waver over whether or not they're satisfied in their marriages to self-centered or cold husbands. In China, however, Lindo Jong knows immediately that she's trapped with a childish partner in a marriage completely devoid of desire.

"AMERICA PROVIDES MORE OPPORTUNITIES FOR FREE THOUGHT, SELF-EXPRESSION, AND MATERIAL COMFORTS."

People in the U.S. live more comfortably than in China. Money and material comforts abound in California, whereas the China of the mother's tales is riddled with hunger, poverty, and hardship. The same women who scrounge together odds and ends to fill their dumplings in Kweilin pat their round bellies in America and coo about how fat they've grown. Women in China wait passively for a house to live in, whereas women in America make their own living arrangements. In China, a girl like Lindo's mother finds herself forced to move from her family's home to her husband's home. In America, a woman like Lena, a trained architect, has the wherewithal to design—and pay for—her own home. In terms of financial clout and material welfare, there's no contest between the smooth sailing of life in America and the continual hardships of China.

Jing-mei's acceptance of her Chinese identity strikingly illustrates the freedom to make choices in America.

The Americans Tan depicts are freer to have and voice their own opinions. As we listen to the sufferings of a young newlywed like Lindo in China, we wonder why she never feels tempted—or rather, how on earth she restrains the urge—to talk back to the older people who oppress and sometimes torment her. In America, the daughters *do* sometimes talk back, as at the end of "Two Kinds," when Jing-mei says that she doesn't have to obey because she's not in China anymore, and not her mother's slave. We may very well feel this same sentiment when reading the stories about being a daughter in China. But in China, such things are never said out loud. Only in America can such opinions be expressed.

And even though the mothers in the novel are sometimes horrified by their daughters' words, they seem to have grown accustomed to the American right of self-expression. The mothers may take offense, but they know that in America they can't punish their offspring for their perceived insults. In "Waiting Between the Trees," Ying-ying St. Clair feels her hand tingling with the urge to slap her daughter Lena for laughing at her mother's mispronunciation of the word "architect"—"arty-tecky," Ying-ying says. But Ying-ying refrains from any violent display of wrath. She says that she holds back because it's too late to change her daughter. But we also feel that Ying-ying refrains because she knows that such behavior is generally unacceptable in the U.S.

Women have the right to choose a husband in America, but not in the mothers' China. In China, Lindo must go marry a man she despises, while in America, the young Lena takes it for granted that she can avoid marrying her schoolmate Arnold, whom she hates. Of course Lena is never expected to marry Arnold in the first place. But the fact that even as a schoolgirl she's convinced of her power to say no to such a marriage points out the difference between the cultures.

Jing-mei's acceptance of her Chinese identity strikingly illustrates the freedom to make choices in America. Jing-mei makes a decision to take over her mother's place at the mah-jongg table and to go to China to visit her relatives. She makes both of these decisions as highly symbolic gestures of a willingness to accept her Chinese ancestry and cultural connections. In her last story, "A Pair of Tickets," Jing-mei recounts how her mother said that Chinese blood simply cannot be denied. Jing-mei spends her childhood rebelling against many aspects of Chinese culture and attempting to turn away from her Chinese blood, though her mother has said it can't be done. In the end, Jing-mei appears to accept her Chinese heritage. She willingly goes to China and embraces her Chinese relatives, and she literally takes over her mother's place at the table. But Jing-mei *chooses* to accept her Chinese identity. No one forces it upon her; she freely takes it on. This kind of freedom of choice toward one's own cultural background would have been unthinkable in China—but in America it strikes us as valuable, even precious.

"NEITHER COUNTRY IS BETTER. BOTH COUNTRIES AND CULTURES ARE EMBEDDED IN THE LIVES OF THE CHARACTERS, AND NO SEPARATION OR COMPARISON OF THE TWO IS EVEN POSSIBLE."

The characters in *The Joy Luck Club* live in a cultural environment that's neither purely Chinese nor purely American—in the Main Street, apple-pie sense of the word—but rather a fusion of both. They've so thoroughly melded their Chinese heritage into modern American culture that probably all the characters, old and young generations alike, would know better than to try to contrast some ideal image of China with the contemporary reality of the United States. They know that real life is too messy and complex.

Tan's women know that the China of their mothers' girlhoods, the China recounted in tales like Lindo Jong's "The Red Candle" or An-mei Hsu's "Magpies," doesn't exist anymore—and perhaps never did, except as airbrushed figments of someone's nostalgic memory. The younger generation is ignorant just by virtue of their American upbringing. In her last story, "A Pair of Tickets," Jing-mei notes that she's never really known what it means to be Chinese. But the older generation also realizes that the China they know may be more faded memory than reality. Exchanging letters with friends and family on the mainland, they grasp that China today must be a very different place from the one the older generation left behind—perhaps even unrecognizable to them. They cannot compare "China" with America, because this dream China doesn't even exist.

Tan's women are aware that they don't fit seamlessly into either traditionally defined American culture or the Chinese culture of their mothers. Ying-ying St. Clair marries a husband whom she doesn't desire and moves into a new apartment that she can't appreciate. Her descent into semi-madness comes across as a symbol of her overall alienation from America. Her daughter, Lena, seems better adjusted to life in the U.S., but Ying-ying says in "Waiting Between the Trees" that Lena's life remains just as empty as her own. Lena, she says, lacks "chi" or spirit, and survives only as a living ghost. But all the women of the younger generation exhibit some personality quirk that shows the impact of their Chinese upbringing on them, and that sets them apart from the American mainstream. Suyuan tells her daughter Jing-mei that being Chinese is in the blood. As a result, she implies, that blood can never be 100 percent American.

Tan's women approach marriage in a way that reflects their membership in two cultures. An-mei Hsu understands that a wife's obligation to stick by her husband, no matter the personal cost, is part and parcel of life in old-world China—but not in contemporary California. An-mei not only permits but quietly encourages her daughter to stick up for herself in her divorce settlement. An-mei delivers her modern feminist advice via an ancient Chinese proverb that compares daughters to growing trees. In this way, An-mei wraps a contemporary American point of view in an ancient Chinese package.

Ultimately, the women of *The Joy Luck Club* put a Chinese spin on American traditions, resulting in behavior neither stereotypically Chinese nor American, but somewhere in between. Living in this middle space, they're unable—and uninterested—in comparing China with America. In the end, they live in a third culture of their own making.

How does Tan portray mother-daughter relationships in *The Joy Luck Club*? Do they come across in a positive or a negative light?

"TAN SHOWS THE CLOSE BONDS OF INTIMACY OF WHICH MOTHERS AND DAUGHTERS ARE CAPABLE. HER PORTRAYAL IS CLEARLY POSITIVE."

Tan shows mothers and daughters to be cut from the same cloth, sharing something that goes deeper than similar cultural upbringing. This connection is in the blood: a daughter doesn't just copy her mother, she *is* her mother, in a deep bodily sense—and this oneness of flesh denotes a positive bond. When the elder members of the Joy Luck Club decide that Jing-mei must go to China to meet her long-lost sisters and tell them their mother's story, Jing-mei initially doesn't believe she knows enough about her mother to take on such a task. She says she just knows that Suyuan was her mother, nothing more. But Jing-mei's response startles the older women. They ask in wonderment how Jing-mei could claim not to know anything about her own mother: "Not know your own mother? . . . How can you say? Your mother is in your bones!" To the older women, a daughter can no more plead ignorance of her mother than she could say she doesn't know her own body. The women say this to reassure Jing-mei: when they say that Jing-mei and her mother share flesh, it's an immensely positive statement.

Jing-mei's intimacy with her recently deceased mother serves as the centerpiece of *The Joy Luck Club*, and though it saddens us, Tan presents it beautifully. Jing-mei initially resists the idea of taking her mother's place at the mah-jongg table, not just because she knows little about the game but also because we sense that she doesn't feel enough of a connection with Chinese culture or her mother's identity as a Chinese woman. Jing-mei is American and young, while her mother was Asian and old—they are incompatible in Jing-mei's mind. Her frequent rebellions against her mother show an urge to separate from her, not to unite with her. But Tan structures *The Joy Luck Club* to bring Jing-mei together with her mother symbolically. By reuniting Jing-mei with her sisters, she says that the mother-daughter relationship must be cherished. Jing-mei is happy in the last scene of the novel partly because she's happy to acknowledge her resemblance to her mother, how alike they look in the Polaroid snapshot taken in China. At the final blissful moment of the novel, a mother and daughter become one.

Mothers sometimes offer spiritual aid to their daughters in unexpected ways. What looks like criticism in the eyes of their sensitive daughters can be a misconstrued offer of help. In this work, the daughters tend to realize only at the last minute that their mothers are on their side. In "Best Quality," Jing-mei recounts her years of frustration at not being able to please her demanding mother. Jing-mei does far less well in her career than Waverly, a successful tax attorney. At a crab dinner, the bitter rivalry between Waverly and Jing-mei surfaces, and Waverly humiliates Jing-mei. When we read that one of the crabs served at dinner is rancid and missing a leg, we expect it to become a symbol of Jing-mei, the "defective" daughter. But Jing-mei's willingness to take the unseemly crab for herself becomes a virtue in her mother's eyes. By the end of the story, the mother finally praises her daughter. Apparent criticism turns to maternal satisfaction in the blink of an eye.

"THERE'S DEFINITELY LOVE BETWEEN MOTHERS AND DAUGHTERS, BUT ALSO DARKER EMOTIONS— JEALOUSY AND MISTRUST—THAT CREATE RIFTS."

We can't idealize the trust between mothers and daughters in *The Joy Luck Club,* for there are too many instances of mothers degrading or manipulating their daughters to satisfy their own ends. The parent-child relationship, while occasionally pleasant, is often barbed. It comes across as a tug-of-war between unfairly matched parties. Mothers and daughters remain in a relentless power struggle, and cruelty and neglect are part of the picture.

Suyuan Woo's shocking abandonment of her twin daughters in China looms over the novel, and we keep it in mind continuously. We can't forget that a case of parental neglect, the abandonment of babies literally on the side of the road, serves as the basic driver of the plot. Since the mothers in the novel often focus on the opposite image of the selfless Chinese mother who would give up anything for the happiness of her children, this instance of maternal abandonment in China haunts us like a dark refrain in a song. When we think of Suyuan as a mother, no matter how much we hear about her good treatment of Jing-mei, we inevitably think of a mother who sacrificed her babies' lives so that she could survive. Much of Jing-mei's difficulty in accepting her mother's past life—an inner struggle that produces much of the drama of *The Joy Luck Club*—is the difficulty of accepting the fact that her mother abandoned her sisters.

An-mei tells a similar tale of maternal abandonment. Her early memory of being burned by hot soup ties in with her memory of her mother leaving the house, not to be seen again for many years. Admittedly, An-mei's

The parent-child relationship, while occasionally pleasant, is often barbed.

mother disappeared no more willingly than Suyuan did: she didn't choose to leave An-mei behind, but was forced to leave when her family believed she had disgraced them. But regardless of the reason, from the girl's perspective it's simple—her mother left her. An-mei's mother repeats this first desertion years later, when she again leaves her girl alone, this time forever. She kills herself to escape her humiliating existence and to get back at her husband. Once again, although the mother feels she has no choice but to abandon her child, no explanation can erase the child's pain.

On the flip side, in instances when mothers stay with their children in *The Joy Luck Club*, their relationship doesn't always prove mutually beneficial or happy. Daughters repeatedly complain that their mothers push them too hard and gripe about the results. A despairing Jing-mei shouts at her mother that America is not China, that she's not her mother's slave. Even taking into account a child's inclination to exaggerate and judging the comparison of childhood to slavery unduly harsh, we still find some truth in Jing-mei's feeling. Between piano practice, chess study, homework, and household chores, the daughters' childhoods are far from carefree.

The mothers in the novel often project their own ambitions onto their daughters, using their children as puppets with which to act out their own thwarted life dreams. Waverly Jong's mother provides a prime example as she trots her daughter around Chinatown to brag about her chess victories. The embarrassed Waverly finally loses patience, bitingly—but with some justification—telling her mother that if she wants to feel proud, she should start playing chess herself. The charge is clear: the daughter feels that the mother uses her to further the mother's own personal ambitions. Lindo Jong's pride in her daughter turns out to be misplaced vanity, which makes Waverly feel slighted.

And in the end, the close bonds between mothers and daughters in *The Joy Luck Club* ensure that any personality flaw in one generation will be passed on to the next, like an inherited disease. The same vaunting boastfulness that the young Waverly despises in her mother ends up emerging in Waverly herself. In "Best Quality," the adult Waverly mercilessly and cruelly belittles her childhood friend Jing-mei, boasting of her fast-track job and her expensive hair salon. In the same way, An-mei Hsu implies that her daughter Rose's inability to appreciate her own value resembles the same trait in An-mei's mother, as if low self-esteem skipped a generation between grandmother and granddaughter. Ying-ying St. Clair also implies that the mother can pass her defects on to the daughter: she says that her daughter, Lena, has no *chi*, or spirit, because she herself has none to give to her. In the end, *The Joy Luck Club* leaves us with the impression that a mother's legacy can be as harmful as it can be beneficial.

"TAN NEITHER GLORIFIES NOR CRITICIZES MOTHER-DAUGHTER RELATIONSHIPS IN THE NOVEL. HER PURPOSE IS SIMPLY TO PAINT A TRUE PICTURE OF THE COMPLEX INTERACTIONS BETWEEN THE TWO GENERATIONS."

Tan shows great sensitivity to the psychology of human relationships and family dynamics. Like other gifted novelists, she aims to uncover the complexity that exists between human beings. Tan holds a mirror up to mother-daughter relationships and shows us what they look like close up. She doesn't pose as an advocate for Chinese Americans, nor as a documentary maker focusing on their problems or flaws. She wants simply to give us the whole picture, including both the good and the bad sides of Chinese-American family life—and of family life generally.

An-mei Hsu's family dynamic illustrates how complex the mother-daughter relationship can be. To start, An-mei, like many women, is both a daughter *and* mother—a fact that already complicates her identity. The stories that feature An-mei present her equally often in both roles, unlike someone like Suyuan Woo, whom we see only as a mother, or Jing-mei, whom we see only as a daughter. An-mei's ties with her mother and her daughter are both burdensome and supportive, critical and inspirational, frustrating and enjoyable.

An-mei's deeply loving mother teaches her a great lesson in remembering her self-worth. In "Magpies," the young An-mei receives a sumptuous-looking pearl necklace from the majestic Second Wife, who tormented her mother when she was married in China. An-mei's mother crushes the necklace in a fit of anger—revealing it to be only a glass

> *"And although we don't speak, I know we all see it: Together we look like our mother. Her same eyes, her same mouth, open in surprise to see, at last, her long-cherished wish."*

fake—and scolds her daughter for being bought off so cheaply. To shift loyalties from a family member to an outsider, in exchange for a trinket or two, is an outrage.

Ironically, An-mei's mother may be guilty of exactly the same mistake. After all, she scandalizes her family by going off with (or being seduced by—we can't tell which) a rich businessman and living in the lap of luxury. An-mei's mother's mansion and fancy clothes may be just another version of the gifts she tells her daughter to mistrust. Her mother doesn't seem to practice what she preaches—which leaves a complex legacy for her daughter. Our ears perk up when An-mei's uncle exclaims that her mother's evil influence is rubbing off on An-mei, for the remark hints at trouble down the road.

An-mei's mother's complicated lessons about money, personal dignity, and compromising one's own values later returns to haunt the women in her family. An-mei's daughter, Rose, has almost the exact same trouble separating material comforts from self-worth. Despite her own personal success and accomplishments, Rose lowers herself to a subordinate position beneath her wealthy doctor husband, Ted. Like her grandmother, Rose devalues her own importance for this seemingly impressive man's sake, until she effectively becomes little more than a servant in a fancy house. And like her grandmother, Rose allows herself to disappear like a ghost. Her grandmother kills herself in a mansion much like the one that Rose is about to lose in an unfair divorce settlement. Both women prepare to give up everything and surrender their claims, all for a man.

Yet within the Hsu clan, it seems that female wisdom and female weakness go hand in hand. The Hsu women pass on low self-esteem from one generation to the next, but they also pass on the strength and wisdom they need to fight it. Together, Tan's mother-daughter relationships show a contradictory mix of characteristics: strength and weakness, insight and blindness, foolishness and wisdom. Just like all human beings, Tan's women aren't cardboard cutouts but three-dimensional characters who are sometimes inconsistent, sometimes in denial, and sometimes unaware of how they hurt the ones they love. But being imperfect by no means makes them bad. Lindo Jong pushes her daughter, Waverly, too hard but also gives her the will to succeed. Ying-ying St. Clair is a passive ghost in her daughter's life but in the end gives Lena the courage to fight like a tiger. Suyuan Woo makes her daughter rebel against Chinese values throughout her life but also leaves her finally able to accept her Chinese identity by going to China and greeting her sisters. Just as in our own families, being harsh and unfair and even cruel doesn't necessarily cancel out love and affection. Tan excels in showing just how complex that knot of family feelings can be.

How does Tan use humor in *The Joy Luck Club*? Does she favor one particular target over any other?

"TAN DELICATELY MOCKS THE OLDER CHINESE GENERATION AS A WAY OF ASSERTING THE DAUGHTERS' BREAK FROM THEIR MOTHERS' CULTURE."

The Joy Luck Club often makes us laugh with its wry humor, much of which comes from the younger generation's gentle but real mockery of the older female characters. While Tan never portrays the mothers as buffoons, she portrays their old-world beliefs, transplanted to a modern setting, as faintly laughable. Like the Chinese swan that the immigration official confiscates in the tale that opens the first section of the novel, the older Chinese immigrants seem at once grandly beautiful and somewhat foolish and out of place. While never denying them respect, Tan nevertheless plays up their comic potential throughout the novel.

Tan often pokes fun at the vanity that lies behind the older mothers' pride in their daughters. The mothers frequently pull the trick of downplaying their daughters' accomplishments in order to brag without being accused of flaunting or boasting—but the obviousness of the strategy is hilarious in itself. At one point, Lindo gravely informs Suyuan that she is lucky indeed. After all, Suyuan doesn't have the burden of polishing all of her daughter's chess trophies, as Lindo does—Suyuan should feel grateful that her own daughter isn't a chess prodigy too.

Not to be outdone, Suyuan fires back with some similarly backhanded praise of her own daughter, complaining that Jing-mei practices the piano so often that she has no time for housework. Of course, she secretly means the opposite: we know that Jing-mei would be released from her household chores if she revealed herself to be a musical genius. Both mothers say exactly the converse of what they mean. Tan expects us to see right through these little mind-games, and we're meant to laugh at how unwittingly transparent they are. We see these older women more clearly than they see themselves, and such a glimpse is always funny.

Often, the target of Tan's gentle jokes is the older women's unwavering and unquestioning Chinese national pride. China remains number one in the mothers' minds, and it seems that no matter how many decades they spend in the United States, they are never able or willing to dislodge China from its pedestal. Their stubbornness on the subject of Chinese superiority is the source of some of the funniest moments in the novel. When the young Waverly Jong asks her mother about Chinese torture in "Rules of the Game," we expect Lindo's answer to be a somewhat embarrassed confession about the cruelty of Chinese warfare and politics—in short, an answer that would compromise the glory of China a bit. Not so. Lindo proudly proclaims that the world finds Chinese torture as praiseworthy an achievement as China's legacy in medicine, painting, or business. Lindo's oblivious defense of human-rights abuse clashes with the liberal position we hear in Tan's modern, northern California voice—and the result makes us laugh.

> The older generation's blunt ways often seem humorously out of place in the laid-back atmosphere of 1980s California.

Sometimes the older women's Chinese pride works against their best interests, and the resulting humor is that of someone shooting herself in the foot. In "Rules of the Game," Waverly recounts how the Jong children received a chess set during a church Christmas gift-giveaway. Mrs. Jong graciously thanks the donor for such an expensive gift, but once at home she scorns the secondhand set, which she imagines must be worthless if someone gave it away for free. Yet the chessboard proves instrumental to her family's honor and joy when Waverly becomes a chess champion. In little more than the blink of an eye, Mrs. Jong's attitude to chess changes from sour dismissal to grave veneration, simply because there's potential for prestige in the game.

The older generation's blunt ways often seem humorously out of place in the laid-back atmosphere of 1980s California. In "Best Quality," Jing-mei describes the feud between her mother and the upstairs neighbors whose cat annoys Suyuan. When the cat goes missing, the tenants insinuate that Suyuan has poisoned it. We realize Suyuan's innocence soon enough, for at the end of the story, Jing-mei looks up to see the tomcat hissing outside the kitchen window. But the upstairs tenants' accusation was not outrageous. The neighbors knew from experience that Suyuan would never pen a polite letter of complaint about an objectionable cat— she would kill the cat and move on to other business. The joke is on Suyuan. Even if we admire her chutzpah in taking the direct approach (or in projecting the personality of someone who does), her cluelessness about local codes of ethics and politeness makes her a somewhat comic figure.

"TAN SPREADS HER HUMOR EVENLY ACROSS BOTH GENERATIONS IN THE NOVEL, FOR SHE OFTEN MAKES FUN OF THE YOUNGER SET TOO."

While the novel's humorous jabs at the older women are more noticeable, Tan also mocks the younger women in a way that is subtler but cuts deeper. The daughters don't do anything as outrageously funny as defend torture or threaten to poison cats, perhaps because they've grown up in American culture and are accustomed to the rules moreso than their mothers. But the daughters nonetheless make amusing errors of judgment concerning their major life choices. Tan allows us to smile at those errors, sometimes with sad irony.

The daughters sometimes take actions and make decisions that are obviously misguided and that are at great odds with their certainty that they know exactly what they're doing. When we read of these, we smile as if we're watching a young animal fall as it learns to walk. The women of the young generation, thoroughly Americanized, believe they know how things work, which makes their mistakes all the more wryly amusing.

In the anecdote that prefaces "The Twenty-Six Malignant Gates," Tan starts off by seemingly mocking a mother but ultimately pokes more fun at the daughter instead. In the anecdote, a mother warns her girl not to ride her bike around the corner, since a scary punishment (listed in an ancient text called *The Twenty-Six Malignant Gates*) will surely befall any child who does. The little girl, full of skepticism toward ancient Chinese lore, thumbs her nose at her mother, shrugs off the advice, and rides around the corner anyway. At this point, we think the joke is on the mother: the misfit immigrant clinging to her old-world superstitions, ignorant of American common sense, comes across as funny. But Tan turns the tables. The daughter immediately falls off her bike as she rounds the corner. Suddenly, the girl's mistaken self-confidence and know-it-all smugness become even funnier than her mother's old-fashioned superstition.

In this way, Tan often feigns mockery of a mother while actually singling out the daughter for the real send-up. After Jing-mei Woo flubs her piano recital, her mother appears faintly laughable when she appears in the living-room to tell Jing-mei that it's four o'clock, time for piano practice—as if ignorant of the disaster at the recital hall. She seems robotic, a stage mother unable to give up the daily schedule of pushing her daughter to success despite the obvious fact that the daughter isn't a prodigy. But years later, Jing-mei's mother, now deceased, has the last laugh. Jing-mei takes a new interest in the piano, has it tuned, and finds that her fingers haven't forgotten how to play. We think back on Jing-mei's mother telling her that she could've been a genius if she had wanted—and we wonder now whether that might indeed have been true. Perhaps Jing-mei chooses to fail in order to refuse to gratify her mother, just as Waverly Jong refuses to gratify her mother when she gives up chess. Jing-mei may have cheated herself out of knowledge of the piano, which showcases the bittersweet irony of being one's own worst enemy.

○　○　○

The subject of money frequently comes up in the novel. Why does Tan focus so much on material wealth?

"TAN USES MONEY AS A RECURRING SYMBOL OF THE GOOD LIFE THAT ALL THE CHINESE IMMIGRANTS ORIGINALLY ASPIRED TO."

Wealth means good things in *The Joy Luck Club*. From the opening pages, Jing-mei describes the Joy Luck Club as four Kweilin ladies who exult in their prosperity. Strikingly, neither Jing-mei nor the ladies who first tell her about the Joy Luck Club's origins in China ever express any guilt or compunction about their luxurious feasts. On the contrary, they exaggerate the luxury, declaring that they simply can't eat another bite as they pat their bellies. We hear the message about money loud and clear: no one needs to apologize for being rich, even in times when others die of hunger.

Both in China and in America, money means power. "The Red Candle" may depress us with its glimpse of Lindo Jong's miserable marriage, but it also shows the extraordinary rights and privileges that the rich can buy. The young husband in that tale would be unable to hide his childishness without his family's wealth and importance. In fact, these things essentially make him a king—if only of a household. Lindo may learn the dangers of arranged marriages, but she also picks up on the benefits of wealth. We feel later, when we meet her success-oriented and upscale daughter, Waverly, that Lindo has passed on that same reverence for wealth. Lindo starts off on the wrong side of the poverty line back in China, and now she makes sure that her daughter will stay on the right side.

Money also brings self-worth. An-mei, for instance, uses a monetary example to teach her daughter, Rose, about the importance of self-confidence and sticking up for herself—she urges Rose to fight for the house in her divorce settlement with Ted. Rose has come dangerously close to surrendering the house, apparently convinced that she's inferior to her husband and that she has no real claim to their common property. An-mei imparts to Rose the idea that the house signifies more than a building. It symbolizes Rose's personal dignity after marriage—the same dignity she has so often sacrificed during the marriage. For Tan's women, wealth counts as more than dollars in the bank account—it brings the ability to stand proud and face the world.

"TAN SEES MONEY AS ONLY ONE PART OF THE BIG PICTURE OF LIFE. IT OFTEN HELPS PEOPLE, BOTH IN CHINA AND IN AMERICA, BUT IT CAN DO HARM TOO."

While wealth brings obvious benefits, it also has the power to corrupt. An-mei's story of her mother's flight from her poor but honorable family to become a rich man's concubine makes us sympathize with the woman in some ways. But to some extent, we may also share her family's horror at the degraded position she accepts in the rich man's mansion. In opting to become fourth wife and third concubine in return for a life of luxury, An-mei's mother subjects herself to fourth-rate status in the household—a degradation that eventually drives her to suicide. An-mei's mother may initially see only the glamour of wealth, and indeed, even the young An-mei exults in her mother's fancy Western clothes and expensive home furnishings. But An-mei's mother's untimely end shows us what we may have felt all along—that finery comes at too high a price.

An-mei's necklace powerfully symbolizes both the allure of wealth and its potential to corrupt and mislead. The seemingly omnipotent Second Wife tries to seduce An-mei away from her own mother, attempting to buy An-mei's favors with a beautiful pearl necklace. For a while we suspect that the trick has worked: the necklace delights An-mei, who feels a warm tenderness for Second Wife as a result of this extravagant gift. But when An-mei's mother angrily crushes one of the necklace beads underfoot, revealing it to be nothing more than cheap glass, we see the lesson clearly. Money can't separate a family or come between parent and child. All the would-be seducers who try to purchase love with wealth are trafficking in fake currency. An-mei's mother, though she may have fallen for the allure of wealth earlier in her life, has learned her lesson about the corruptive power of money the hard way.

Money corrupts people and relationships in America just as readily as in China. Wealth naturally affects marriages in a very different way in the United States, where wives can more easily earn their own income. Nonetheless, it can prove just as detrimental. Whereas some of the stories in China depict a rich man terrorizing a poor wife, Lena St. Clair's marriage illustrates how money can endanger a relationship not through inequality but through too much equality. Lena and her husband Harold split every little expense, essentially reducing their marriage to a financial arrangement, a balance sheet. Harold believes—or for a while makes Lena believe—in this division of expenditures. But in fact he practices nothing more than a modern version of what the petty male tyrants did to their wives back in China: manipulating them for their own uses. Lena's mother confirms her suspicions about her daughter's marital problems when she sees the couple's expense sheet taped to the fridge. This telltale account sheet symbolizes money's ability to rot out even a seemingly equal marriage.

A Reluctant Role Model

Although some see Amy Tan as an emblem of the Asian-American community, she disdains being pigeonholed as an author who represents only one group.

AMY TAN HAS NEVER CLAIMED to be a role model for Chinese Americans, or to be the final word on them. Nonetheless, her work has done much to shift a generation's perceptions of Chinese Americans. With her breakthrough novel, *The Joy Luck Club*, now taught in the curriculum of a huge number of schools across the United States, schoolchildren write essays on her work and share their feelings about it. Yet Tan declares that the primary aim of her novel was never to teach anyone about Chinese culture. She aimed instead to explore human relationships and family ties above all—the cultural aspect is only secondary.

Tan's chosen course has brought her wild success in both literary and financial terms. She has published a number of novels that both critics and ordinary readers have embraced. After the release of *The Joy Luck Club* in 1989, Tan followed up with *The Kitchen God's Wife* (1991), the children's book *The Moon Lady* (1992), *The Hundred Secret Senses* (1995), and *The Bonesetter's Daughter* (2001). Tan's work has been translated into over twenty languages worldwide, and awards began appearing soon after her first novel was published. *The Joy Luck Club* won the National Book Critics Circle Award and was a finalist for the 1989 National Book Award.

Like *The Joy Luck Club*, all of Tan's work has followed the heritage of Chinese immigrants to the United States. Her novels study family and personal relationships, usually in the intimate words of a first-person narrator. *The Hundred Secret Senses* explores cultural differences between Asia and America by delving into the interconnected lives of two half-sisters, the fully Chinese Kwan and the half-Caucasian Olivia. Kwan believes in ghosts—or what Tan prefers to call "yin people." Olivia doesn't, at least at first. Kwan succeeds in convincing Olivia and her husband to believe in supernatural forces by the end of the novel. In this way, China teaches America a thing or two in most of Tan's novels. In *The Bonesetter's Daughter*, the discovery of a mother's lost life story in China revives her daughter's vitality in America.

Tan's work doesn't shy away from the graphic—some viewers objected to the murder of an infant in the film version of *The Joy Luck Club*. Indeed, Tan's own family background contains its share of trauma. Born on February 19, 1952, Tan was fourteen when she lost both her brother and her father. Her sixteen-year-old brother, accused of plagiarism in a high-school English class (he had allowed a friend to look at his paper), fell into a depression, and died only a few weeks later of a brain tumor. Tan's mother would later insist that the brother's death came as a result of the plagiarism charges. In a tragic coincidence, Tan's father died of the same ailment—a brain tumor—in that same year.

Tan's mother experienced horrors on her own side of the family as well. After witnessing firsthand the suicide of her mother (Tan's grandmother) many years earlier, she never fully recovered from the shock.

Story, language, memory

Tan on whether she is comfortable as a role model: "No. Placing on writers the responsibility to represent a culture is an onerous burden. Someone who writes fiction is not necessarily writing a depiction of any generalized group, they're writing a very specific story. There's also a danger in balkanizing literature, as if it should be read as sociology, or politics, or that it should answer questions like, 'What does *The Hundred Secret Senses* have to teach us about Chinese culture?' As opposed to treating it as literature—as a story, language, memory." (*Salon* interview, 1995)

Before her suicide, that same grandmother had been a victim of rape in China—an assault that Tan used as the basis for the terrifying rape scene in *The Kitchen God's Wife*. Indeed, one of Tan's relatives criticized her for including that scene in her second novel, considering it a disgrace to the memory of her grandmother.

Moreover, as in *The Joy Luck Club*, there are abandoned children in the Tan family tree. Tan's mother was forced to leave three daughters back in China, much like *The Joy Luck Club*'s Suyuan, who abandons her two daughters while fleeing the Japanese invasion. The ghosts and painful memories that fill Tan's work may have originated in her life story.

Tan started writing early, at the age of eight, winning first prize in a library contest for an essay called "What the Library Means to Me." The prize was a transistor radio. Tan claims that her interest in storytelling came from listening to her father's sermons. He was a Baptist minister who would often entertain his children by reading to them aloud. After attending school in Montreux, Switzerland—where life as a middle-class child surrounded by rich kids was an eye-opening experience—Tan finished a master's degree in linguistics from San Jose State University. She then worked as a bartender and child counselor before returning to writing as a profession, penning speeches for business executives at IBM and Apple Computer. But in 1987, finding herself unfulfilled by this work, Tan turned her hand to fiction writing, producing the manuscript of *The Joy Luck Club*.

Despite Tan's rather unusual upbringing, she did experience some of the pressures to succeed that Asian parents often instill in their American-born children. Tan once noted in an interview that her parents expected her to become a doctor by profession and a part-time concert pianist by hobby. She also felt the cultural alienation that other Asian-American children have felt growing up—for a certain period, she counted herself the only Chinese girl in her school. Tan has explained that the conflict of ideas resulting from such a culturally displaced childhood taught her to ask a lot of questions, to approach life with an inquisitive spirit.

Today, Tan enjoys the life of an established and prolific writer. She lives in San Francisco and New York City with her husband, Lou DeMattei, whom she married in 1974, and her Yorkshire terrier, Babbazo (also called "Mr. Zo"). She co-produced and co-wrote the screenplay for the acclaimed 1993 film version of *The Joy Luck Club*.

From China to Chinatown

Despite the universal nature of its stories, *The Joy Luck Club* is inextricably tied to Chinese and Chinese-American history.

THE JOY LUCK CLUB CUTS A SWATH ACROSS time and space, from early twentieth-century China to 1980s California. To grasp the full cultural importance of the novel, it helps to go back a bit and retrace the history of Asian immigrants in the United States. This historical review may seem tedious or unnecessary to some readers. We may wonder why we should think about Chinese-American history when reading *The Joy Luck Club* any more than we should dwell on Irish-American history when reading *The Great Gatsby*, simply because its author, F. Scott Fitzgerald, was Irish-American.

But Tan's novel, concerned as it is with the intersection of past and present, calls for some thinking about the past. *The Joy Luck Club* spans more than a hundred years of history in its narrative and, along the way, illuminates the huge changes that take place in that period. The novel makes us think about the differences in marriage and women's status and encourages us to draw historical comparisons between Shanghai in 1918 and San Francisco in the 1980s. In short, Tan forces us to become amateur cultural historians when we read her novel.

In the twenty-first century, many of us might not think twice about Asian Americans' gradual immersion into the culture of the United States. And we may not be as aware of the social injustices Asian Americans have suffered. In part, this lack of awareness may stem from the fact that Asian

Americans have in many ways become assimilated to mainstream American culture—arguably more so than any other recent immigrant group after the Europeans.

America did not always embrace its Asian population. Throughout much of the twentieth century—around the time An-mei's mother's tale was unfolding—many white Americans viewed Asian Americans as little more than anonymous faces. When huge numbers of Chinese men were shipped to the West Coast for hard labor, excavating mines and laying railroad lines, American officials often treated them as little more than beasts of burden. Some scholars believe that the Chinese dish called chop suey, a legacy of this bleak period of Asian-American history, was originally a derogatory reference to the scraps and leftovers that Chinese workers often had to eat. And because the vast majority of educated white Americans were completely unfamiliar with Chinese languages, the communication gulf between Asians and the rest of America yawned wide for many decades.

With this great lack of understanding, white Americans in the nineteenth century often used Asian immigrants as scapegoats for a host of complaints. They often stereotyped Asian Americans as shifty or treacherous. In the 1920s, urban legends of the Chinese white slave trade and opium addiction ran wild. We even see these urban legends resurface today: just one example is the film (now a musical) 1920s flapper comedy *Thoroughly Modern Millie*, with its interludes set in an ornately decorated Chinese lair.

In the 1940s, negative stereotypes against Asian Americans persisted in a different way, as many Japanese Americans were discriminated against

Cultural connections

As we see in *The Joy Luck Club*, many Chinese immigrants to the U.S. have been careful to ensure that their American children maintain a familiarity with and respect for Chinese culture. Just as many Jewish immigrants to the U.S. have expected their children to attend Hebrew school, many Chinese parents in San Francisco's Chinatown have had their children attend the Nam Kue Chinese School, founded in 1919 and given its own building in 1925. Today, the school offers classes in Chinese language and culture to more than 800 students.

and even interned in camps during World War II. Racism flourished as many white Americans conflated "the enemy" with their countrymen of Chinese and Japanese descent. Then, in the 1950s, the Cold War-era stigma of Communist China rubbed off on many Chinese Americans who tried to maintain links with their families in Asia.

In the later decades of the twentieth century, Asian Americans gradually began to enjoy a higher social status in the United States. One milestone was the Vietnam War of the 1960s and 1970s, which many young Americans opposed and which deeply changed American attitudes toward Asia and Asians generally. Although the war sometimes stirred up American prejudices against Asians—in the story "Half and Half" in *The Joy Luck Club*, for instance, we see the Chinese-American Rose patiently explain to her boyfriend's white mother that she's not Vietnamese—it made others rethink their ideas and stereotypes of unquestioned American superiority.

Economic advances had a great impact on public attitudes toward Asian Americans as well. The Asian economic boom of the late 1970s and 1980s prompted many white Americans to shed their negative stereotypes of Asian Americans and to respect their Asian-American counterparts as talented businesspeople. At about the same time, many second-generation Asian-American students, profiting from their parents' insistence on hard work and the value of education, began to pour into prestigious universities and lucrative careers. Tan touches on this phenomenon in *The Joy Luck Club*, in which the daughters are successful—tax attorneys, writers of advertising copy, architects.

As this newly raised status of Asian Americans took root, America began to see it reflected in art, in literature, in popular culture, and in business. More than was ever dreamed possible a hundred years earlier, Asian Americans were finally being heard.

A Literary Landmark

The Joy Luck Club has moved from the bestseller lists to a firm foothold in book clubs and syllabi around the world.

WHEN *THE JOY LUCK CLUB* APPEARED in 1989, the first novel of a then-unknown writer, Chinese-American literature was already an established—if not high-profile—literary field. A decade earlier, the talented Chinese-American novelist Maxine Hong Kingston had published *The Woman Warrior* (1976) and *China Men* (1980), her semi-biographical works on Chinese immigrants in California. These books paved the way for Tan's fiction, not only in telling tales about Chinese-American life but also in using a very personal first-person narrator—Kingston's "I" meets us on intimate terms, just as Tan's does. Kingston also mixes Chinese mythology with realistic prose, evoking fantastic dream imagery similar to the imagery Tan uses in "The Red Candle" and "Magpies."

The Joy Luck Club, though, attained a popular success that Kingston's earlier novels never quite reached. Tan's first novel became a bestseller, striking a chord with readers across the country—not just those in communities with large Asian-American populations. Tan's mixture of feisty American rebelliousness and respect for Chinese ancestors, her ability to poke fun at the Chinese elders at the mah-jongg table while driving home their wisdom, won over a huge readership in the United States and in other English-speaking countries. And not only there: in the past decade, *The Joy Luck Club* has been translated into over twenty languages.

Released at a time when many in the United States were eager to represent minority voices in literature—and in the literature curricula of secondary schools—*The Joy Luck Club* became a top choice for the new reading lists. Easy to read but challenging to discuss, the book offered a new perspective not only on women but on Chinese Americans as well.

A staple in eighth-grade English classes, it also stands up under the scrutiny of high-powered critics.

Despite Tan's acknowledgements in interviews of her discomfort with her role as representative of the Chinese-American community, her novel is often taught as an introduction to the culture of that group. But many other teachers have chosen the book simply as a beautifully written and moving story of family life—something to which students of any background can relate.

Whatever the reason for the novel's rise to popularity, it has become a staple in English classes across the nation. Even the most cursory Internet search reveals a plethora of eighth-graders diligently reading and writing about *The Joy Luck Club* for school. At the university level, the book is equally well represented, discussed within a more sophisticated framework of literary analysis, where it stands up well under the scrutiny of high-powered critics. The combination of depth and accessibility that makes Tan so special has assured her novel's popularity on a wide range of educational levels.

Many critics focused on the mother-daughter relationships that are at the center of *The Joy Luck Club*. The title of Orville Schell's review of the novel in *The New York Times Book Review*, "Your Mother Is in Your Bones," shows the importance of this generational theme to many readers. Schell praised Tan's novel for its truthful representation of generational bonds as well as generational conflicts, for its portrayal of the ways in which mothers and daughters can squabble and bicker but never forsake their love and kinship. John Skow, writing in *Time* magazine, similarly lauds Tan's portraits of female strength in the novel and her hard-nosed, realistic depiction of power dynamics among women.

Other critics examined Tan's vivid representation of Chinese-American life and its complex relationship to white America. Rhoda Koenig's review "Heirloom China" in *New York* magazine saw this minority aspect as the central theme of the novel. Joyce Maynard's *Mademoiselle* piece—a crucial article that exposed Tan's novel to a broad female reading public—reviewed *The Joy Luck Club* alongside *The Temple of My Familiar* by Alice Walker. The title of Maynard's review, "The Almost All-American Girls," explored the connections between Tan and Walker as minority voices in American literature.

Critics also appreciated *The Joy Luck Club* simply for its fine writing. Schell, in *The New York Times Book Review*, expressed relief that Tan's novel never preaches or becomes overly didactic, and thus avoids the moralizing pitfalls that in his opinion have marred many other novels. In the same vein, *Newsweek*'s Dorothy Wang praised *The Joy Luck Club* for its subtle refusal to pound commentary into our heads and for Tan's way of showing us what the characters see without adding distorting interference of her own.

Of course, like any literary work that achieved such broad fame so quickly, *The Joy Luck Club* also has its share of detractors. Some Asian American critics worried that readers took Tan's novel far too widely as a holy text on the Chinese-American experience—despite Tan's repeated insistence in interviews that she never claimed to represent Chinese Americans as a whole. Julia Oh, in an essay called "Why 'Joy Luck' Brings Me Misery," objected strenuously to the novel's inclusion in school curriculums across the country. She complained about Tan's portrayal of unrealistically "meek" Asian-American women and asserts that *The Joy Luck Club* in no way reflects the experiences of the average Asian American in the United States.

For the most part, though, readers continue to love *The Joy Luck Club*. One sure sign of its triumph with the American public was its transformation into a Hollywood film in 1993, which Tan herself co-produced (with Oliver Stone and others) and co-wrote. Directed by Wayne Wang, the film won largely positive reviews, and many claimed that it was one of the most successful literary adaptations in recent memory. Some viewers found the sixteen stories too complex to be transferred easily to the screen, and others objected to the lofty dialogue used in the film, which the online critic James Berardinelli found "too poetic to be real." But millions of people all over the world saw the film, securing *The Joy Luck Club*'s place as one of the prominent American cultural narratives of the last decades of the twentieth century.

Other Books of Interest

Tan's novels are part of a growing canon of literature about cultural and generational conflict in America, past and present.

○ ○ ○

BY AMY TAN

THE BONESETTER'S DAUGHTER
(Putnam, 2001)

A novel about memory and identity, Tan's fourth fictional work gives us the perspective of a Chinese-American woman struggling to come to terms with her mother's Alzheimer's disease. Among her mother's papers she discovers an entire secret history of her mother that she never before suspected.

THE HUNDRED SECRET SENSES
(Putnam, 1995)

A tale of two half-sisters, the fully Chinese Kwan and the half-Caucasian Olivia, who each come to accept the other's different perspectives on life. Tan's descriptions of the "yin people," or ghosts, bring Chinese folklore to California, and Olivia and her husband come to believe in these ghosts by the end of the story.

THE KITCHEN GOD'S WIFE
(Putnam, 1991)

Perhaps the most graphic and disturbing of Tan's exposés of the horror of domestic life in China and the unfair distribution of power between men and women. This novel interweaves fact and fiction as the author retells the story of her grandmother's rape. Tan manages to make this lurid tale lighthearted in spots and full of her characteristic wry humor.

BY OTHER AUTHORS

LITTLE WOMEN
by Louisa May Alcott (1869)

Little Women is the classic American novel about growing up as a girl, with all the ups and downs of mother-daughter relations. Tan echoes Alcott in her portrayal of girlish errors of judgment, in the absence of strong father figures, and in the daughters' struggle to reconcile maternal devotion with their desire for independence. Like Tan, Alcott presents us with four very different daughters who complement one another in their disparities as much as Tan's daughters do in *The Joy Luck Club.*

A YELLOW RAFT IN BLUE WATER
by Michael Dorris (Holt, 1987)

Dorris's first novel interweaves the stories of three Native American women: a daughter, her mother, and her grandmother. The three different voices speak volumes about the potential for misunderstanding and conflict across generations, reminding us that perspective is everything and that there's never only one "true" version of a story.

THE WOMAN WARRIOR
by Maxine Hong Kingston (Knopf, 1976)

Set in Stockton, California, Kingston's memoir endures as one of the preeminent Asian-American immigrant stories of the twentieth century. Kingston writes richly about her life among the white American "ghosts" around her and the China of her ancestors' "talk-stories." Kingston's strongly feminist and often bitter viewpoint has made *The Woman Warrior* a highly controversial and widely read work.

CHINA MEN
by Maxine Hong Kingston (Knopf, 1980)
Kingston's other classic tale of Chinese-American immigrant life focuses on the hardships endured by her grandfather, who came to the U.S. from China to work on "Gold Mountain," the mythic Chinese name for the American gold rush in the 1850s. *China Men* shows the contributions—and sacrifices—that this man and thousands of Chinese men like him made to the fledgling American mining and railroad industries.

BELOVED
by Toni Morrison (Penguin, 1988)
This haunting, poetic novel tells the story of an African-American slave woman, Sethe, who resorts to an unspeakable deed to save her daughter from the horrors of slavery. Just as in *The Joy Luck Club*, we see in *Beloved* that a mother's love can take mysterious forms, and that the secrets of the distant past are not always easily buried.

DRAGONWINGS: GOLD MOUNTAIN CHRONICLES
by Laurence Yep (HarperCollins, 1975)
A Newbury Honor book, this children's novel introduces us to the eight-year-old Moon Shadow Lee, who travels from China to join relatives in San Francisco. Though lighthearted and whimsical, *Dragonwings* also illuminates more serious topics, including the strained relations between Chinese and Caucasian people in early twentieth-century California.